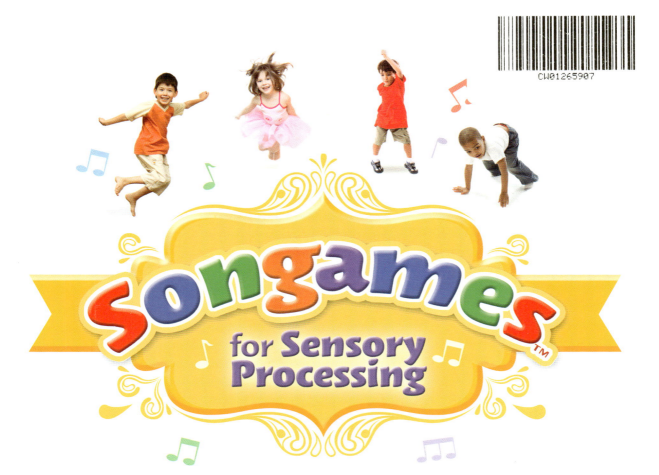

Songames™ for Sensory Processing

by Aubrey Lande, MS, OTR, Bob Wiz,
Lois Hickman, and friends

A proud imprint of Future Horizons
Arlington, Texas

SONGAMES for Sensory Processing
All marketing and publishing rights guaranteed to and reserved by:

A proud imprint of Future Horizons

1010 N Davis Drive
Arlington, TX 76012
(877) 775-8968
(682) 558-8941
(682) 558-8945 (fax)

E-mail: *info@sensoryworld.com*
Web site: *www.sensoryworld.com*

©2010 Sensory World
©2001, 2002 Sensory Resources, LLC
©1999 Belle Curve Records, Inc

Cover and interior design by Monica Thomas for TLC Graphics,
www.TLCGraphics.com.

All photos courtesy of: *iStockphoto.com*

All rights reserved.

No part of this product may be reproduced in any manner whatsoever
without written permission of Future Horizons, Inc, except in the case of
brief quotations embodied in reviews.

ISBN: 978-1-935567-07-3

The creators, producers, and distributors of this product disclaim any liability or loss in connection with the exercises and advice herein. Always consult your physician when seeking to make informed medical decisions.
Always use with proper supervision.

Co-produced by Bob Wiz and Aubrey Lande. Engineered by Mark Derryberry and Bob Wiz. Recorded at Fanfare Recording Studio in Golden, Colorado, and Seahorse Recording in Boulder, Colorado. Mastered at Fanfare in Lakewood, Colorado.

Acknowledgments

Thanks to Art Lande for his incredible musical contribution, once again.

To the parents of the kids on this recording, for being so supportive.

To Mary Darlington, Marcy Marchand, and Benjamin Buren for helping to make the dream real.

To all of the people kind enough to give us feedback during the testing phase.

To our families, friends, clients, and students, from whom we learn and grow.

To all of the musicians on the recording.

And finally, thanks to you!

Contents

The Circle Form Concept 6
How to Get the Most Out of Songames for Sensory Processing 8

CD #1 13

Balance Circle Form (18:36) 14
1. Twelve Chinese Secrets (4:18) — 15
2. A Waiting Game (2:03) — 18
3. Musical Chairs (3:59) — 19
4. Hum-Along (4:20) — 21
5. Sweet Life (3:50) — 23

Message Circle Form (14:06) 24
6. Deep-Pressure Chant (1:05) — 25
7. Makin' Pizza (2:05) — 28
8. The Hot-Dog Game (4:15) — 31
9. Mouth Toys (2:10) — 33
10. The Basics of Friendship (4:23) — 35
    Friendship Survey — 37

Bob's Circle Form (16:59) 38
11. Jeopardy (1:16) — 39
12. The Reptilian Factor (2:55) — 40
13. Forest Stump (4:07) — 42
14. I Like Bananas (4:59) — 43
15. Calm One (3:36) — 47

CD #2 49

Lois's Circle Form (16:35) 50
1. Radio W.A.K.E.-UP! (3:07) — 51
2. The Clothing Quiz (2:16) — 52
3. Dip Down (4:05) — 54
4. The Nose Knows (3:30) — 56
5. Love and Kindness (3:30) — 59

Aubrey's Circle Form (20:06) 60
6. Glider Rider (5:35) — 61
7. Fine-Motor Samba (2:59) — 62
8. Give a Little Yodel (2:49) — 64
9. Slowing Down (2:39) — 65
10. Mama Loves Me (5:53) — 66

References 67
Glossary 70
Resources 73
About the Authors 80

The Circle Form Concept

Prior to putting these Songames into a final order, we asked many friends and colleagues to review the material and give us feedback. Darlene Lorainne, a friend of ours who is a brilliant teacher, had some useful suggestions regarding how to cluster the Songames into "mini-curricula." She told us of a concept she'd developed over the years—something she calls "circle forms."

A typical circle form lasts 15-25 minutes. Darlene uses breath as a metaphor for a good circle form. The initial activity in one of Darlene's circle forms is like an in-breath, opening the heart and soul, lifting the eyes, and expressing one's self. By the end of the circle form, the activities should be geared toward helping children calm, center, and prepare to transition out of the form and into their day.

Borrowing directly from Darlene's concept, we have organized the Songames into five distinct circle forms. Each one has a slightly different flavor, yet each one comprises five Songames on the basis of the following sequence:

1. *Transition In:* These Songames set the tone, or mood, of the circle form.
2. *Instructive songs:* Children listen to the song lyrics of these Songames and follow along, with minimal-to-moderate independence and minimal-to-moderate modeling cues.
3. *Heavy Work:* These Songames encourage proprioceptive or organizing play, often requiring modeling and verbal guidance by the supervising adult.
4. *Sensory-Motor Activity:* These Songames encourage oral-motor play, olfactory play, respiratory play, or graded movement.
5. *Calming Activity:* These Songames are designed to bring the circle form idea to a close, gently preparing children to shift to an unrelated activity, such as a purely academic task or story time.

The circle forms are:

Balance Circle Form: The Balance Circle Form is about learning to explore action and stillness and learning how to find balance.

Message Circle Form: Though more verbal and linguistic than the other forms, this eclectic form is also embedded with important things to learn. By internalizing the messages in this form through rehearsal and repetition, children can begin to gain conscious, cognitive awareness of the skills necessary for decreasing tactile defensive reactions, enhancing proprioceptive play, and acquiring the skills necessary for having and being a friend.

Bob's Circle Form: This form was hand-picked by Bob Wiz for kids who need lots of rhythm and "heavy work" kinds of play to feel grounded and centered. It will especially help kids who like a lot of stimulation, be it aural, tactile, visual, or even internal.

Lois's Circle Form: The intent of Lois's Circle Form is to help kids awaken their bodies and minds, infusing themselves with a good attitude and good energy. The rocky transitions of a child's day are made smooth with gentle humor and gradually more energetic engagement with "the things that need to be done."

Children enjoy a smooth "musical landing" to bring them from focused, thinking play to a calm, quiet place once again. This circle form might be useful to play at the child's bedside as part of a wake-up routine.

Aubrey's Circle Form: "Sensory modulation is the tendency to generate responses that are graded in relation to incoming sensation" (Lai et al). Kids who struggle with generating the "right" response to incoming sensations can have a difficult time in situations that demand a high frequency of correct responses to incoming sensations. Children are not supposed to freak out when they hear the bell to change classes or have a meltdown if their orange juice has too much pulp in it. However, the kids we love often have a difficult time generating the right response to certain types of stimuli because their perception of incoming sensation is different. Sounds are too loud or too soft, and smells are too strong or too weak. Some children even have difficulty knowing exactly where their body is in space because their relationship with gravity is challenged. Aubrey's Circle Form is intended to help children experience myriad musical inputs and translate the cues into graded responses (actions). This is the perfect circle form to try with kids who tend to be too responsive to incoming sensation. The circle form flows from big, playful movements, creativity, and innovation, to a slower, more peaceful and relaxing state.

How to Get the Most Out of Songames for Sensory Processing

Songames for Sensory Processing was created by licensed therapists and professional musicians as a way to add music to a child's "sensory diet." A sensory diet is a set of activities designed for a person to do throughout the day to help him reduce stress and keep his nervous system in a state of balance. Over the years, the creators of this program refined and enhanced the ability to reach children through music and movement.

Here are some tips that may help you know "what to do and how to do it" with regard to using this music at home, in school, or just about anywhere. Once you become familiar with the activities and lyrics of each Songame, try the variations suggested to spice it up a bit and keep things interesting.

General Tips

People often ask us, "How do you introduce the Songames to children?" Should they be presented as therapy (something to do) or as music (something to listen to)? Each child is different, and each listening situation will require a unique approach.

To help you determine how to introduce Songames into a child's life, we recommend that you first listen to both CDs in their entirety. This will help you better gauge which Songames will most benefit each child and his or her specific needs.

Listen to them while driving around town or working out. Select the Songames you like the most, and think about the ones your kids will like. Do a little homework. Review the booklet and get a sense of your intent.

This is especially important for classroom environments. Teachers, occupational therapists, certified occupational therapist assistants, music teachers, gym and adaptive

physical education teachers—what is your intent? If your desire is to have every child participate fully, then some kids may need a little more help understanding "what to do and how to do it."

Depending on the child and the situation, you may:
➤ Have children listen to the Songames in a small group.
➤ Send the Songames home with the children so they can practice in a "safe" environment. Get parents, siblings, and babysitters involved! This may be especially important for children with sensory defensiveness issues.
➤ Have the child do the song in front of a mirror at first. Asking children to do them in pairs can be very hard on children who are visually defensive or can't handle a lot of eye contact.
➤ Be fully aware of the perimeter of the environment you are working in. Children with sensory defensiveness may have difficulty successfully participating in activities if distractions are too great.
➤ If you can't control the environmental distractions, help the children feel more composed by doing rhythmic and proprioceptive activities, such as playing "The Hot-Dog Game," "Forest Stump," or "Give a Little Yodel."
➤ Start out in a smaller group and don't insist on eye contact.
➤ Encourage "creative interpretation," but model the actions along with the kids so they know what the movement expectation is.

Being Prepared

If your intent is to get a group of 30 kids playing along to the "Fine-Motor Samba," then you'll need to have a clear idea of what you're trying to do. You may want to think of props (scarves, crayons, paper, etc) to have in place before the activity starts.

If you're planning to use a mixture of Songames from several different circle forms, first make a playlist with the track numbers of the songs you select. When a Songame ends, move quickly to the next desired CD track. Kids get fidgety when a structured activity, such as playing a Songame sequence, becomes unstructured by the need to cue the next song.

Repetition and Routine

Children learn through repetition and rehearsal because this gives them a sense of constant structure they can count on. If an activity is fun, goofy, fulfilling, and rewarding, children will quickly identify with the intent and start to incorporate the lessons into their lives more easily. Successful introduction of the Songames in this recording can lead to several inspired methods for getting a child's or classroom's attention. With this hurdle cleared, exceptional results will come more quickly and frequently.

Individual and Home Use

Parents have had great success incorporating Songames into their home routines. Again, we always recommend that caregivers listen to the Songames once or twice before playing them for their children.

The Songames are novel and entertaining, but encouraging "call and response" play happens easiest when the Songames are first acted out for the child to see. If an adult knows what to do and how to do it, that knowledge can help the child embrace the play actions easier.

Kids love fun routines, so we suggest capitalizing on this affection. Making a list of the Songames that your child wants for his or her wake-up routine can make a world of difference on a cold school-day morning.

Some parents start their child's day with "Radio W.A.K.E.-UP" and "The Clothing Quiz." Others have found that starting with "Glider Ride," followed by "Reptilian Factor" and "Forest Stump," is the right combination.

Setting out clothes the night before and having clear goals for what grooming activities are expected by the time the music finishes can be useful in helping kids become more organized and independent in the morning. You may wish to expand on the idea of using Songames to help make the organization and definition of everyday tasks more fun for your child.

Consider developing routines for the following:
➤ Waking up
➤ Dressing
➤ Activities of daily living
➤ Meal preparation
➤ Meal cleanup
➤ School preparation
➤ School commute
➤ Use before and after homework
➤ Use before and after chores
➤ Use after dinner
➤ Use before bed and/or as part of the bedtime routine

You'll notice that most of this list consists of things to do before an activity, as well as ways to help retain one's sense of organization after an activity is complete.

One of the hallmarks of Sensory Processing Disorder (SPD) is an inability to initiate, organize, and follow through on routine tasks in an efficient and well-planned manner. Knowing this, we can understand how preparing the mind and body for routine tasks can help children remember the sequence of an activity and how to enact the steps involved.

Often, parents struggle with helping their kids make and keep friends (ie, "social competence"). Children can find learning how to make friends confusing, as well as how to play with them once they've got some! Sharing your child's favorite Songames with a friend or two can help the kids develop an icebreaker game.

Lastly, if your child loves these Songames but after a while starts to yearn for something new and different, try one of our other award-winning, activity-based musical projects. For younger children, ages 3-9, you may want to try "28 Instant Songames" or "Marvelous Mouth Music." Slightly older children, ages 5-12, may identify more with "Danceland."

Balance Circle Form
1. Twelve Chinese Secrets
2. A Waiting Game
3. Musical Chairs
4. Hum-Along
5. Sweet Life

Message Circle Form
6. Deep-Pressure Chant
7. Makin' Pizza
8. The Hot-Dog Game
9. Mouth Toys
10. The Basics of Friendship

Bob's Circle Form
11. Jeopardy
12. The Reptilian Factor
13. Forest Stump
14. I Like Bananas
15. Calm One

Balance
Circle Form

The Balance Circle Form is about learning how to explore action and stillness and finding balance.

RUN TIME 18 minutes, 36 seconds

Twelve Chinese Secrets

RUN TIME 4 minutes, 18 seconds   **ARRANGEMENT BY** Lande/Lande

VOCALS & MUSIC BY Aubrey Lande—lead vocals. Megan Wolstenholme—kid vocals. Art Lande—piano.

Children can self-regulate by remembering to "play hard!"

Variations:

♪ This Songame would be good for starting a class or group meeting, doing before breakfast at camp, or playing with daycare groups.

♪ Each child in a group can demonstrate something or share something that makes him or her feel good.

♪ As part of a circle activity, this Songame could help children develop more self-awareness and serve as an introduction to self-regulation.

♪ You could help the child make his or her own "fidget box," filled with a few favorite things. Make sure you include objects for the mouth, hands, and the whole body, after you learn what your child needs for his or her sensory diet (see the Glossary for more information). This fidget box can be part of helping the child develop an awareness of what he or she might need for self-regulation.

♪ Learn Sarah's "Twelve Chinese Secrets" so you and the kids can practice this child-friendly tai chi any time you need a movement break. Don't forget the animal noises you can make while enacting the 12 animal forms. Encourage kids to make noises from their bellies—not shrill, high-pitched noises. Loud is okay, but shrill can be hard on the ears.

TWELVE CHINESE SECRETS (continued)

Sarah went to her doctor to ask her this question
When I can't do my homework, what's your suggestion?
"Your mind works its best when your body feels great
Try my Twelve Chinese Secrets, they'll help change your state"
She caught on so quickly to the twelve golden tidbits
Her grades got much better and so did her friendships
Everyone wanted to know what she'd done
To do all her homework and make life more fun!

Sarah's parents and teachers were simply astounded
By the wide range of changes from just feeling "grounded"
They stood in a circle and asked her to share
Her knowledge so obvious, yet oddly so rare
When my clothes itch
Or I'm anxious
Or just not myself and mad
I've got to remember to play hard, then hey!
I don't feel so bad...

CHORUS *encourage kids to follow along to the movement instructions given by the performer:*

Take an enormous breath
Whinny like a horse
Walk sideways like a crab *(the lower and slower the better)*
Bob your head like a bird *(injury prevention tip: keep it gentle—avoid extremes of movement)*
Be as tall as a giraffe
Hop, hop, hop like a frog, ribbit
Squeeze! *(hunch shoulders, flex arms, squint, squeeze every part of your body, release)*

Swim like a dolphin *(have kids say this lyric as if they are talking fish)*
Go crazy like a monkey
Push your hands together
Stretch!
Smile!

Sarah went to her doctor to ask her a question
When I can't do my homework, what's your suggestion
"Your mind works its best when your body feels great
Try my Twelve Chinese Secrets
They'll help change your state!"

Balance Circle Form **17**

A Waiting Game

RUN TIME 2 minutes, 3 seconds	ARRANGEMENT BY Lande
VOCALS & MUSIC BY Amy Jacobs—kid vocals. Art Lande—piano. Concept—Aubrey Lande and Bob Wiz.	

Make waiting fun! Many children with SPD and regulatory disorders struggle with impulsivity and frustration tolerance. Learning the concept and the verbal cues associated with waiting is an important skill. A child's voice gives the cues, which is easier to tolerate than having a grown-up person tell you what to do!

Variations:
- ♪ Move with the music and listen for the cues to stop, freeze, then move again.
- ♪ Use whole-body movements and control, or just use the mouth, eyes, feet, elbows, fingers, and knees.
- ♪ Draw with a variety of media, stopping and starting with the music and cues.
- ♪ This song can be used as children line up to go to recess or to catch the bus.
- ♪ This Songame makes fabulous music (and cueing!) for Freeze Tag.

Musical Chairs

RUN TIME 3 minutes, 59 seconds **TRADITIONAL ARRANGEMENT BY** Lande/Johns
VOCALS & MUSIC BY Geoff Johns—frame drum. Sound effects—Aubrey Lande and Mark Derryberry.

This is a new, noncompetitive twist on an old familiar game.

Variations:

- ♫ Don't remove any of the "landing spaces."
- ♫ The "chairs" can be beanbag chairs, paper plates, cushions, carpet pieces, balls, a piano bench, rocking chairs, a barrel, or an inner tube.
- ♫ Move with the drumbeats and find a place to sit when the drumming stops.
- ♫ Have kids play musical instruments along with the rhythm (you can't make a wrong note, just "free play" to the rhythm. The important concept is to start when the drumming starts, try to keep in rhythm, and stop when the drumming stops.)
- ♫ A circle or group of kids can take turns doing a funny dance in the middle of the circle during each of the rhythmic sections.
- ♫ Play "follow the leader" dancing! The leader leads the group around the room in a speed appropriate to the rhythm. Switch leaders during each section or let kids take a longer turn leading.
- ♫ Move in any way the music makes you feel! Bounce, hop, skip, march, somersault, twirl, creep on your hands and knees, or dance gracefully.

Balance Circle Form

MUSICAL CHAIRS (continued)

Door opens
Sounds of applause

Slow walking beat
Chinese gong sound
Bell cue *(stop moving!)*

Medium walking beat
Bowling pins sound
Bell cue *(stop moving!)*

Fast walking beat
Tennis volley sound
Bell cue *(stop moving!)*

Jogging beat
Cash register sound
Bell cue *(stop moving!)*

Running beat
Organ music
Bell cue *(stop moving!)*

Running beat
Shuffling cards sound
Bell cue *(stop moving!)*

Jogging beat
Horsey horn sound
Bell cue *(stop moving!)*

Running beat
Kissing sound
Bell cue *(stop moving!)*

Jogging beat
Sneeze sound
Bell cue *(stop moving!)*

Fast walking beat
Chime sounds
Bell cue *(stop moving!)*

Slow walking beat
Organ music, applause
Door closes

Hum-Along

RUN TIME 4 minutes, 20 seconds **ARRANGEMENT BY** Lande/Wiz/Burhoe/Freeman

VOCALS & MUSIC BY Aubrey Lande—lead vocals and hums. Ravi Freeman—kora. Ty Burhoe and Bob Wiz—hums.

The heartlike beat, with the hum-along sound, soothes, calms, and focuses. Humming and singing are shown to produce the mood-altering neurochemical serotonin. Serotonin helps us feel happy and balanced.

Variations:

- ♫ Feel the audio speakers with your hands, face, or feet.
- ♫ Hum along with the sounds; use your hands to feel vibration on your face, throat, or chest.
- ♫ Rock in a hammock with the sounds.
- ♫ Swaddle the child in blankets. He may choose to be wedged in with pillows or with his favorite stuffed animals.
- ♫ At bedtime, use after the rituals of bath, teeth-brushing, and story time—whatever your family routines involve. Rituals are comforting and organizing.
- ♫ Groups of children can listen to this song together by lying down on the floor, face up, with their heads toward the center of the circle. Have kids hum or "tone" to the song.
- ♫ The advanced version of this Songame is to hum energy into different body parts. You can do this by thinking of a part of your body (like your hands or your heart) and then humming into that mental image. This is a healing meditation used for centuries by people from a variety of cultural and religious traditions. With practice, you can learn to direct the sounds quite precisely and actually feel them resonate in different parts of your body. There is no right or wrong way to do this—it's personal. Give yourself permission to have fun, explore, be a little wild, maybe even feel foolish. Intention is of the utmost importance. Sending yourself healing sounds infused with light and love can be very powerful. Trust your intuition. We know from experience that this can help us feel more centered.

HUM-ALONG (continued)

Try experimenting with different vowel sounds (ahhhs, eeehs, ooohs, etc). You may discover that different sounds have different effects. Listen to a baby to hear how she expresses different emotions. If some sounds make you feel "spacey," make sure you take time to do a "grounding activity" before driving your car or engaging in activities that require a different type of attention. Grounding activities incorporate some sort of pressure and the use of your muscles. For example: Try pushing a vacuum cleaner, carrying heavy boxes, jogging, or jumping up and down with your hands on top of your head. Enjoy!

So, come along
And hum along
Hum on this song along
So, come along
Just hum along
Hum on this song along
Hum to the heartbeat
The heartbeat of life

Sweet Life

RUN TIME 3 minutes, 50 seconds **ARRANGEMENT BY** Freeman
VOCALS & MUSIC BY Ravi Freeman—kora. Ty Burhoe—tabla.

This is a Songame to help your child get ready for an activity that requires focus.

Variations:
- ♪ Use before doing homework.
- ♪ Use before helping with family routines, like setting the table or preparing a lovely (no matter how simple) centerpiece for the table.
- ♪ This song can enhance and increase the pleasure of doing everyday chores and encourage a little beauty in the "mundane."
- ♪ Dance with the children.
- ♪ This is a fun song to accompany a "scarf dance." Long, brightly colored scarves or streamers are engaging, alerting, and visually stimulating. Scarves can also be helpful with "crossing the midline" exercises.

Balance Circle Form

Message
Circle Form

Though more verbal and linguistic than the other forms, this eclectic form also embeds important lessons. By internalizing the messages in this form through rehearsal and repetition, children can begin to gain conscious, cognitive awareness of the skills necessary for decreasing tactile defensiveness, enhancing proprioceptive play, and acquiring the skills necessary for having and being a friend.

RUN TIME 14 minutes, 6 seconds

Deep-Pressure Chant

RUN TIME 1 minute, 5 seconds **ARRANGEMENT BY** Lande
VOCALS & MUSIC BY Aubrey Lande—vocals.

A cheer for the home team! Research shows that children learn with significantly more efficiency and retention when information is taught through rhythmic song coupled with simple gestures. This chant is really a mnemonic device to help kids remember that if they're feeling itchy and wiggly, there might be a sensory explanation. This song can teach kids how to do two important things:

1. Recognize and change something about their environment (clothing, lighting, sounds, sights, smells) that is overloading their nervous systems.
2. Use deep pressure to help their nervous systems inhibit the irritating sense of inability to screen sensory stimuli—what one child termed "the traffic jam in my head."

Again, there are countless ways to safely apply deep pressure, including isometrics (alone or in pairs); jumping jacks or other calisthenics; stretching; jogging; chores that require lifting, pushing, or pulling; swinging; arm wrestling; bouncing on a mini-trampoline; or jumping up and down with your hands on your head. Keep it safe with adult supervision.

Message Circle Form

DEEP-PRESSURE CHANT (continued)

Take off that itchy sweater and we'll all feel better when we use deep pressure to calm!
Once again y'all

CHORUS

Ahumme chicky chicky wha
Ahumme chicky chicky wha
Ahumme chicky chicky wha
Ahumme chicky chicky wha
Ahumme

Take off that itchy sweater and we'll all feel better when we use deep pressure
...to organize
...to focus
...to ground
...to relax
...to calm
...to focus
...to center
...to ground
...to relax

Variations:

Songame equation: Fill in the blank with your own activity, paired with a movement action, so you can generate new ways to play this Songame.

_____
(ACTION TO ALLEVIATE DISCOMFORT)

and we'll all feel better
when we use deep pressure to
_____
(DESIRED FEELING/STATE)

For example:
Action to alleviate discomfort:
- ♪ Air out that stuffy room
- ♪ Turn down that loud TV
- ♪ Turn off fluorescent lights
- ♪ Turn off that buzzing light
- ♪ Clean up that cluttered room
- ♪ Get some structure in your day
- ♪ Create some cool routines
- ♪ Get to sleep by _____
  (BEDTIME)

If you use any of these lines, you may choose to keep the secondary line or find an appropriate rhyme. You may also substitute any of the sensory-diet activities for "use deep pressure to _____"
(DESIRED OUTCOME)

For example:

Clean up that cluttered room
And your sense of peace will swoon
When you use calm spaces to relax

Create some cool routines
Using story boards and scripted scene
Planning is a muscle we must use to _____
(DESIRED OUTCOME)

Cheers and chants are terrific mnemonic devices, in that the rhyming and the rhythm make them easy to recall. Try and create pantomime gestures to go along with the cheers, and you'll double your kids' capacity to retain and reference learned material.

Makin' Pizza

RUN TIME 2 minutes, 5 seconds	**ARRANGEMENT BY** Lande/Rugenstein
VOCALS & MUSIC BY Doc Rugenstein—congas and percussion. Aubrey Lande—lead and harmony vocals. Bob Wiz—voice of "Obo." Kid chorus composed of Zahara and Mahalia Porter, Robert-Josef and Samuel Heitzer, and Alizé Marchand.	

Kneading dough is a work activity that will help your child feel more organized. This can be a great family-centered activity.

Variations:
- ♪ Make homemade dough, pie dough, or cookie dough. Use your hands to knead it together.
- ♪ Dance, stomp, or push the dough in time to the music.

Aubrey: Obo, let's make a pizza!
Obo: Pizza, pizza! Yes!

Making pizza, making dough
Put in the flour and the water
Making pizza, making dough
Put in the flour and the water
Knead the dough
Knead the dough
Everybody knead the dough

Making pizza, making dough
Put in the flour and the water
Making pizza, making dough
Put in the flour and the water
Knead the dough
Knead the dough
Use persistence and knead the dough

Making pizza, making dough
Put in the flour and the water
Making pizza, making dough
Put in the flour and the water
Knead the dough
Knead the dough
Squeeze and pull and push the dough
Knead the dough
Roll the dough
Squeeze and squish and push
　　the dough

Making pizza, making dough
Put in the flour and the water
Making pizza, making dough
Put in the flour and the water
Squeeze the dough and pull the dough
　　and stretch it so it's sooo long
And then punch it down
Very good
Punch it down, yeah

And roll it in a little ball,
Perfect Obo!
Making pizza, making dough
Put in the flour and the water
Making pizza, making dough
Put in the flour and the water

Obo: May I have some pizza?

MAKIN' PIZZA (continued)

When I first wrote these lyrics, Bob wondered why I would use a word like "persistence," which is educational jargon. I explained that oftentimes, grade reports contain the word, such as, "Annie demonstrates poor persistence in tasks that require turn-taking."

Kids with special needs have a hard time learning how persistence feels. Generally, we all know the sensation of doing something enjoyable for a long period of time, but persisting through something that is repetitive—that's more elusive.

Understanding what it feels like to "persist" rather than "give up" will help your child feel good about herself. Without being too much of an army sergeant, set realistic goals. "I want you to pretend to roll and squeeze pizza dough until you hear Obo's voice" or "...until the end of the song."

Not only can this help kids develop the neuromuscular skills to improve handwriting and other fine-motor skills, but it also helps them improve frustration tolerance. Most importantly, it helps them to internalize the process of setting realistic goals and achieving them. Keep it fun, though. If you use real dough, a purposeful focus is possible.

—*Aubrey*

The Hot-Dog Game

RUN TIME 4 minutes, 15 seconds   **ARRANGEMENT BY** Lande/Lande

VOCALS & MUSIC BY Amy Jacobs—kid vocals. Aubrey Lande—lead vocal. Art Lande—piano.

This Songame connects a child's need for proprioception (see the Glossary) with humorous, creative play.

Variations:
- ♪ This is a nice "calm-down" for a child who just can't get enough deep pressure.
- ♪ It can be used as a transitional activity, as one game or activity ends, and the children need to get ready for something new.
- ♪ Before excursions to the supermarket, this game could be used to help coax the child into a calmer state and help the child imagine the "condiments" that need to be purchased.
- ♪ Have your child make his or her favorite sandwich.
- ♪ Keep adding condiments for increasing deep pressure.
- ♪ Use siblings as condiments!
- ♪ Have siblings make their favorite sandwich, too. After they make their favorite sandwich, unroll the sandwich by racing to the nearest wall.
- ♪ Take turns with family members pushing and squeezing, always respecting the child's wishes about the amount of pressure and contact.
- ♪ Get the whole family involved!

First you get a hot-dog bun, bunny
First you get a hot-dog bun
Then you're lying on your tummy on a hot-dog bun, bunny
This isn't silly, this is serious

Next you put the lettuce on, bunny
Lovely-looking lettuce on
So you're lying on your tummy on a hot-dog bun
With some lettuce on your back but you're still not done
This isn't serious, this is silly

Let's get tomatoes now, bunny
Red and ripe and yummy

THE HOT-DOG GAME (continued)

So you're lying on your tummy on a hot-dog bun
With lettuce on your back, but you're still not done
Tomatoes on top, but we just can't stop!
Wait...
Hold on...

Push, roll *(repeat five times)*
Push and roll along
The rest of this song
Push and roll *(repeat five times)*
The rest of this song

Push around the hot dog
Squish and mush the hot dog
Be very careful how you play
This game is played in a really safe way, bunny
Push
Roll
Push

Squish
This is the hot-dog game we play
It's going to help us feel all right all day
We roll and squish and push and squeeze
Help our bodies and our minds be in harmony
'Cuz that's important, bunny
This isn't silly, this is serious

Tomatoes come off and the lettuce is put away
And the hot-dog bun which gave us some fun yeah it's put back for the day
Tomato goes off
And the lettuce is put away
And the hot-dog bun which gave us some fun is put back, Jack
That's right
Yeah, yeah, yeah
Have a great day!

Mouth Toys

RUN TIME 2 minutes, 10 seconds	**ARRANGEMENT BY** Lande/Lande
VOCALS & MUSIC BY Aubrey Lande—vocals. Art Lande—piano. Bob Wiz—nose flute and kazoo.	

NOTE *Always use adult supervision to make sure the deep pressure is comfortable and safe for the child.*

Exploring sensations and sounds in your mouth helps you get ready for speech. (For more vocal sound play, try our "Marvelous Mouth Music," "Songs for Speech Therapy & Beyond," which we created in collaboration with the amazing speech therapist Suzanne Evans Morris, PhD, CCC-SLP.)

Variations:
- ♪ Use in school before music class or before speech therapy.
- ♪ Use as part of a home program for speech exercises.
- ♪ Get friends and family together to make your own songs with mouth toys.
- ♪ Keep your favorite mouth toys in a treasure box and always try to add new ones.
- ♪ Keep a list of your favorite sounds.
- ♪ Create your own personal "dictionary" of invented words.

Play along with me
This song will set you free
Everybody make some noise
With mouth toys
Mouth toys

Puff and make 'em snuffle
Whiff and poof the whistle
Everybody make some noise
With mouth toys
Mouth toys

We've got whistles
And we've got kazoos
Party makers
And who knows how to use this one?

Play along with me
Everyone will feel so free

MOUTH TOYS (continued)

Everyone make some noise
With mouth toys
Mouth toys

Okay, take a solo!
That's right.
(musical interlude)

We've got whistles
And we've got kazoos
Party makers
School's out, let's make some noise!

Everybody play along
Everybody do it right, wrong,
    who cares!
Have some fun
With mouth toys
Yeah mouth toys
Everybody make noise with mouth
    toys now!

The Basics of Friendship

RUN TIME 4 minutes, 23 seconds | **ARRANGEMENT BY** Lande/Lande

VOCALS & MUSIC BY Based on the Stony Mountain School's Friendship Survey (used with permission). Aubrey Lande—vocals. Art Lande—piano. Bob Wiz—chimes. Kid chorus composed of Zahara and Mahalia Porter, Robert-Josef and Samuel Heitzer, and Alizé Marchand.

This Songame encourages an awareness of what it takes to be a friend and make and keep friendships.

Variations:

- ♫ Use for "circle of friends" gatherings.
- ♫ Use for playgroups or daycare groups.
- ♫ Use at campfire groups, when everyone is sitting together.
- ♫ Use to begin a conversation about friendship.
- ♫ Use as a round, like "Row, Row, Row Your Boat…"
- ♫ Have your child write down all the characteristics that he or she likes in a friend, or let your child dictate to you and watch as you write them down.
- ♫ Ask your child what he or she does to keep a special friend.
- ♫ Have your child act out a situation where he or she did a special thing for a friend.
- ♫ Some of the special friends may be animals, or even plants or imaginary characters.
- ♫ Ask what special care these friends need—you may be surprised. Besides being fun, encouraging imagination helps set the groundwork for creative problem-solving.
- ♫ Make your own "Friendship Survey."

Trust each other
Help each other
Play together
Stay loyal, too
Share with each other and
Do fun things together
A friend's someone you can talk to
    who will listen to you… *(repeat)*

To have a friend is to be a friend
To have a friend is to be a friend
Simple are the basic ways that we all
    make friends
To have a friend is to be a friend

Message Circle Form

THE BASICS OF FRIENDSHIP (continued)

To have a friend is to be a friend
Simple are the basic ways that we all make friends

Trust each other
Help each other
Play together and
Stay loyal, too
Share with each other
Do fun things together
A friend's someone you can talk to who will listen to you... *(repeat)*

To have a friend is to be a friend
To have a friend is to be a friend
Simple are the basic ways that we all make friends
To have a friend is to be a friend
To have a friend is to be a friend
Simple are the basic ways that we all make friends

Make new friends, but keep the old
One is silver and the other's gold

(Repeat and sing in a round until the end of the song)

Friendship Survey: What Is Most Important in a Friendship?

The fourth-grade class at Stony Mountain School, Stony Mountain, Manitoba, Canada, interviewed and surveyed 198 people on what is most important in a friendship. They interviewed their families and friends. They also asked people on the Internet to join in their project. The students heard from a variety of places, as close as Winnipeg to as far away as England and New Zealand. They also heard from a number of places in the United States.

Then the students compiled all the responses, of which there were 67 different ones. They categorized some of the responses that fit into the same category (eg, shopping, playing in the sandbox, having sleepovers, and going to the movies were placed in the category of "doing things together").

The students found that the 10 most important aspects of a friendship are the following:

1. Friends can trust each other.
   (24 responses)
2. Friends help each other.
   (23 responses)
3. Friends do things together.
   (18 responses)
4. Friends are loyal to each other.
   (14 responses)
5. Friends are honest with each other.
   (13 responses)
6. A friend is someone who you can talk to and who listens to you.
   (12 responses)
7. Friends share with each other.
   (8 responses)
8. A friend is there in the good times and the tough times.
   (5 responses)
9. Friends never judge you. They accept you for who you are.
   (5 responses)
10. Friends have fun together.
    (4 responses)

Bob's
Circle Form

This form was created by Bob Wiz for kids who need lots of rhythm and "heavy work" play to feel grounded and centered. It especially helps kids who like a lot of stimulation—be it aural, tactile, visual, or even internal.

RUN TIME 16 minutes, 59 seconds

Jeopardy

RUN TIME 1 minute 16 seconds **ARRANGEMENT BY** Griffin; arrangement by Lande
VOCALS & MUSIC BY Art Lande—piano. Bob Wiz—clave and woodblock.

Here's a chance for kids to move, hop, and transition from one activity to another.

Variations:
- ♫ Add "heavy work" (proprioception) to this song to help your child get more organized.
- ♫ Move heavy objects with the beat.
- ♫ Throw heavy beanbags at a target while listening to the beat.
- ♫ Sing along, clap hands, and make up a finger dance.
- ♫ Use this Songame for playing "statue" games. Have kids "strike statue poses" during the silence and "hold" the poses while playing 5-10 seconds of this song.

Bob's Circle Form **39**

The Reptilian Factor

RUN TIME 2 minutes, 55 seconds	**ARRANGEMENT BY** Wiz
VOCALS & MUSIC BY Bob Wiz—udu (clay pot drum), bells, keyboard, shakers, drum machine, and intro vocals. Aubrey Lande—voice of "Lester the Leaping Lizard."	

Increase body awareness as you crawl, slide, and slither like a lizard.

Variations:
- ♪ Crawl through tunnels, under chairs, and under mattresses.
- ♪ Slide toward a target.
- ♪ Try sliding over different surfaces to vary the sensory experiences.
- ♪ Explore the use of different media (crayons, markers, shaving cream, sidewalk chalk, etc) to write your name or draw designs.
- ♪ For more fine-motor and visual-motor play, guide a small stuffed animal through the actions of the story.

Once there was a lizard who lived upon a rock
Under the hot desert sun
Working on his tan
Dreaming of the sand
Doing what lizards love to do
You can be a lizard
It's really very fun
Changing colors in the midday sun

Hello, my name is Lester the leaping lizard
And I'm so glad that you've come to visit me
In my home in the Mojave Desert
It's hot here but there's sand as far as the eye can see
Come play with me as we do here in the desert
And to play here in the desert

SONGAMES for Sensory Processing

What we do is we lie down on our tummies
We stretch our arms and our legs out and we begin to slide
Sliding on the sand dunes all the way down to the bottom of the hill in the desert
Let's slide

We are sliding on our bellies
Sliding through the slippery sand
It is hot but we have got
A lot of crawling that we want to do
In the desert

Crawling and stretching is so nice when the sand is warm on your belly
This is my favorite thing to do
I love to make big circles in the sand with my hands
Don't tell anybody but sometimes I like to write my name in the sand
Do you?

Forest Stump

| **RUN TIME** 4 minutes, 7 seconds | **ARRANGEMENT BY** Wiz |

VOCALS & MUSIC BY Bob Wiz—drums, percussion, bull-roaring, vocals, and frog recording. Sound effects—Bob Wiz, Lois Hickman, and Mark Derryberry. Kid chorus composed of Robert-Josef and Samuel Heitzer, Zahara and Mahalia Porter, and Alizé Marchand.

This Songame is good for gross-motor skills, vocalizing, rhythmicity, cooperation, self-regulation, respiratory play, and more! Once again, keep it safe with proper adult supervision. This is a work song, or labor chant, based on the popular children's game "tug-of-war."

In our version, we eliminate the competitive aspect and have two groups of kids pulling on a single rope in time to the rhythm. Encouraging the kids to mimic the vocal sounds of "hun" and "ugh" encourages deeper respiration and phonemic vocalization. Substitute names or create a counting game to broaden the sound play.

This game can also be played with a single child (or group) pulling on a rope securely attached to an appropriate stationary object. They can pretend they are pulling a tree stump from the forest floor. They may even pretend to be the elephants heard in the song!

Variations:
- ♫ Do push-ups.
- ♫ Play tug-of-war.
- ♫ Do isometrics against each other's hands or feet.
- ♫ Pretend you're pushing a wall down.
- ♫ Lean against the wall with your back and push.
- ♫ Use imaginary play—tell a story as the children do heavy, pushing work, or slow, heavy, stomping around a pretend swamp.

I Like Bananas

RUN TIME 4 minutes, 59 seconds   **ARRANGEMENT BY** Lande/Wiz

VOCALS & MUSIC BY Aubrey Lande—vocals. Bob Wiz—backup vocals, drums, and percussion. Mark Derryberry—sound design.

Playing with sounds takes the scare out of having to say things "right."

Variations:
- ♪ Use a straw, especially when drinking thick liquids. This helps a child focus and calm.
- ♪ Use different kinds and shapes of straws for variety. Aquarium tubing makes a good straw, too.
- ♪ Sip thicker substances, such as pudding, applesauce, milkshakes, fruit shakes, or "slushies," for more proprioceptive resistance.

This Songame is also good for:
- ➤ Oral-motor play
- ➤ Respiratory play
- ➤ Developing group skills
- ➤ Imaginative play
- ➤ Rhythm play
- ➤ Gross-motor imitation
- ➤ Developing body-language and feeling identification

If my mouth was a house
It's a very, very noisy place
Un, hungh, yeah, yeah
Well if my house was a mouth
It's a very, very noisy place
Un, hungh, yeah, yeah
Cuz' there's a lot a lot of sounds
In a very little squishy space
Oh whoa, whoa, oh whoa, whoa
There's the sound of the slurpy

Bob's Circle Form

I LIKE BANANAS (continued)

Who slinks through the kitchen
There's the sound of the grumpy
Whose kind of down and dumpy
And as always as with any other place
There are cows and orangutans all
 over the place
And the orangutan goes:
"I like bananas"

Umm, yummm, you do? Umm,
Well if your mouth was a house it's a
 very, very noisy place
Un, hungh, yeah, yeah
If your house was a mouth it's a very,
 very noisy space
Un, hungh, yeah, yeah
So play along with me and we'll party
 with our goofy faces
Yes, here we go:

Thick milkshake with a skinny
 little straw
See how much your mouth can draw
I'll count to one *(sucking liquid through
 a straw sound)*
But we're not done
Let's count to two *(suck/gulp
 sound twice)*
But we're not through

Hey, let's count to three *(suck/gulp sound three times)*
Ah, wait for me!
Let's count to four *(four suck/gulp sounds)*
Let's do some more—wow! Holy smokes!
That's the spirit! Can we hear it a little louder?

NOTE *Suck-swallow-breathe noises encourage oral-motor food play. Adult supervision is* **very important.**

Cheeks puffed up like a chipmunk can
Pop your cheeks with both of your hands
(Have child fill cheeks with air and purse lips to create a "balloon" face, then "pop" cheeks by gently pushing index fingers against the taut cheek skin)
(repeat action)

Pretend your mouth is filled with stuff
And try to say the alphabet
A B C D E F G
Pretend your mouth is very, very small
And try to say the alphabet, barely moving it at all
A B C D E F G
(jibber-jabbering)

If my mouth was a house
It's a very, very noisy place
Un, hungh, yeah, yeah
If my house was a mouth
It's a very, very noisy place
Un, hungh, yeah, yeah
Cuz' there's a lot a lot of sounds
In a very little squishy space
Oh whoa, whoa, oh whoa, whoa

There's the sound of the slurpy
Who slinks through the kitchen

I LIKE BANANAS (continued)

There's the sound of the grumpy
Whose kind of down and dumpy
And as always, as with any
    other place
There are cows and orangutans all
    over the place
And the orangutan goes:
"I like bananas"

NOTE *Some children cannot perform the oral-motor tasks encouraged in this song at the speed suggested.* **Do not compromise safety!** *Rather, turn off the player and generate your own activities based on what the child can manage safely and enjoyably.*

Calm One

| **RUN TIME** 3 minutes, 36 seconds | **ARRANGEMENT BY** Wiz |

VOCALS & MUSIC BY Bob Wiz—keyboard, water, cello, vocals, and percussion. Lois Hickman—drum.

This is a "warm musical bath," good for transitioning in or out of quiet time.

Variations:

♪ Imagine the "sound" of sunlight flickering on ripples in a pond.

♪ Imagine your own story; pretend you're at sea, swimming or diving, or back in your mother's womb. You could even be out in space−or let the children pretend they are a school of fish! The possibilities are endless...remember to include a lot of different senses in your imaginings.

♪ Listen quietly with headphones when appropriate.

Bob's Circle Form **47**

Lois's Circle Form
1. Radio W.A.K.E. -UP!
2. The Clothing Quiz
3. Dip Down
4. The Nose Knows
5. Love and Kindness

Aubrey's Circle Form
6. Glider Rider
7. Fine-Motor Samba
8. Give a Little Yodel
9. Slowing Down
10. Mama Loves Me

Circle Form

The intent of Lois's Circle Form is to help kids wake their bodies and minds, infusing themselves with good attitudes and good energy. The rocky transitions of a child's day are made smooth with gentle humor and gradually more energetic engagement with "the things that need to be done." Children enjoy a smooth "musical landing" to bring them from focused, thinking play to a calm, quiet place once again. This circle form might be useful to play by the child's bedside as a wake-up routine.

RUN TIME 16 minutes, 35 seconds

Radio W.A.K.E.-UP!

RUN TIME 3 minutes, 7 seconds	**ARRANGEMENT BY** Lande/Rugenstein/Buren
VOCALS & MUSIC BY Benjamin Buren—the voice of "Ben Jammin." Doc Rugerrstein—congas. Aubrey Lande—the Yabadabadoers. Aubrey Lande, Bob Wiz, and Lois Hickman—finger snappin'.	

Kids can wake up happy! This song helps children get ready for their day, with a playful "alarm clock" announcement from Ben Jammin' of Radio W-A-K-E. This Songame might be used in combination with the gentle wake-up of "Calm One" to create a customized wake-up call. Use an alarm clock with a CD player and set it to wake your child up to this Songame.

Wake up yabadaba daba yaba daba daba
Wake up yabadaba daba yaba daba daba do
Breathe yabadaba daba yaba daba daba
Breathe yabadaba daba yaba daba daba do *(repeat)*

Squeeze your legs yabadaba daba yaba daba daba *(repeat)*

Squeeze your arms yabadaba daba yaba daba daba do *(repeat)*

Push your hands yabadaba daba yaba daba daba *(repeat)*
Push your hands yabadaba daba yaba daba daba do *(repeat)*
Stretch up yabadaba daba yaba daba daba *(repeat)*
Stretch up yabadaba daba yaba daba daba do *(repeat)*
Stretch long yabadaba daba yaba daba daba *(repeat)*
Stretch wide yabadaba daba yaba daba daba do *(repeat)*

Make a funny face... *(repeat)*
Funny face funny dance... *(repeat)*

Lois's Circle Form

The Clothing Quiz

| **RUN TIME** 2 minutes, 16 seconds | **ARRANGEMENT BY** Lande/Lande |

VOCALS & MUSIC BY Aubrey Lande—vocals. Art Lande—piano. Bob Wiz—voice of announcer. Mark Derryberry—boingy sound.

Thinking ahead about what to wear can make the whole day easier!

Variations:

- ♪ Promote sequential thinking!
- ♪ Try it with your child's morning routine, when you're making a sandwich, and even at nighttime. This will allow your child to be more in control of his daily routine and help him or her to plan out familiar and new activities.
- ♪ Use after "Radio W.A.K.E.-UP!"
- ♪ Use as part of the bedtime ritual—getting ready for the next day and laying out clothes that will be worn the next day.
- ♪ Make it into a pantomime game for circle time.

It's the clothing quiz!
Here's a silly game you can shout
    your answer
When I sing this question and you
    hear this sound—"boing!"
What do you wear under what
    you're wearing?
Tell me what the first thing is that
    you put on?
What do you wear under what
    you're wearing?
You wear, "boing!" *(name item
    of clothing)*

That's right!
You know what to do
You put your underwear on!
Good guess, you know how to dress, yes
Good guess, you know how to dress!
I knew you would know the answer

This is s silly test, I said, okay!
After the underwear what comes
   next dear?
What kind of clothing do you put on?
Choose from the following list
   of options:
      Hat
      Vest
      Bathing suit or pants
Hmm? I wonder what you're going
   to choose?

Huhh...that's right!
You put on your pants!
Good guess you know how to dress, yes
Good guess, you know how to dress
I knew you would have the answer
This is a silly test I said, okay!
After your underwear and after
   your pants
What would be the perfect thing to
   put on next?
Think..."boing!" *(name item of clothing)*

Unhungh! Something to keep
   you warm...
Sometimes it comes in cotton
   or flannel
Sometimes it's got the name of a
   baseball team written on it
You put it over your head, put your
   arms through it
That's right, it's a tee shirt!
Good guess, you know how to dress, yes!
Good guess, you know how to dress
I knew you would have the answer
This is a silly test, I said, okay!

After the underwear and after
   the pants
And after your tee shirt what
   comes next?
We're going to end this quiz with
   one question.
What goes on your feet?
"boing!" *(name item of clothing)*

Lois's Circle Form **53**

Dip Down

RUN TIME	4 minutes, 5 seconds	ARRANGEMENT BY	Wiz
VOCALS & MUSIC BY	Bob Wiz—keyboard and lead vocals. Aubrey Lande—backup vocals.		

This is an irresistible dance tune! The whole family may want to join in the swaying, twirling, and humming, from babies held in your arms to siblings, parents, and grandparents. The upbeat feeling of "Dip Down" can help increase body awareness, improve your mood, improve balance skills, and encourage imagination. It serves as an icebreaker for any gathering or a way to wind down before saying "good-bye." It gently helps refocus if used between activities.

Variations:

- ♫ Move only your head, shoulders, arms, eyes, or fingers.
- ♫ Shift your weight from side to side, sway, dip down, reach up, and twirl around the room.
- ♫ Have a target for the child to reach toward. Gradually increase the height of the target. A frame drum works great for this activity.
- ♫ Have the child reach for his or her favorite animal. Imagine that you're saving the animal from a windstorm or from someone who is too rough.

Dip down, dip deep down
Dip down, dip deep
(repeat five times)

Swing side to side, side to side,
 side to side
Swing side to side, side to side,
 side to side
Swing like a tree in the breeze
 blowing free
Swing side to side, side to side,
 side to side

Plant your feet like you have roots in
 the earth
And swing side to side, side to side,
 side to side

Reach way up high, so very high
Reach way up high, up into the sky

Reach up higher now
Then you've ever, ever reached before
La la la la

Reach way up high
Up into the very sky
Reach way up high
So very high

An instrumental passage follows, which is good for dipping, swinging, reaching, and free dancing. This is also a good time to engage in "play and response" games, where one person is identified as the "leader" and others imitate. Or, divide the group into partners, and take turns leading and following.

Dip down, dip deep down
Dip down, dip deep
(repeat five times)

Swing side to side, side to side,
 side to side
Swing side to side, side to side,
 side to side

Plant your feet like you have roots in
 the earth
Swing side to side, side to side,
 side to side

Reach way up high, so very high
Reach way up high, up into the sky
Reach up higher now
Than you've ever, ever reached
 before
La la la la

Reach way up high
Up into the very sky
Reach way up high
So very high

Lois's Circle Form

The Nose Knows

RUN TIME 3 minutes, 30 seconds	**ARRANGEMENT BY** Lande/Lande
VOCALS & MUSIC BY Aubrey Lande—lead vocals. Art Lande—piano. Bob Wiz—backup vocals. Amy Jacobs—kid vocals.	

Become more aware of that wonderful sense that's so important in mood and memory!

Variations:

♫ Smell is the most powerful way to affect the frontal cortex of the brain. Smell can be used for alerting and attending, as well as comforting and soothing. Aromatherapy is a compelling body of information on how to use "olfaction" to enhance function.

♫ As you walk or bike around town or in the country, notice the different smells. Do different smells make you feel different ways or remind you of places or events?

♫ A smell game can be fun! Gather different aromas from the kitchen, such as vanilla, lemon, chocolate, peanut butter, apples, oranges, and bananas. Close your eyes and guess what each one is before you look at it or taste it.

♫ See if you can remember the order that the scents were presented in after you play a smell game, or perhaps suggest some foods they're in or even how they can be used. These sorts of variations can be a good memory wake-up, as well.

56 SONGAMES for Sensory Processing

Have you ever thought about…
    smelling?
Think about it!
It's kind of fun…
Imagine the smell of chocolate…yum!
Doesn't that smell scrumptious!

Let's make up a game about…
    smelling?
How would you do that?
I'll show you how!
Find the real scents or imagine them
And follow along…

Breathe in
Chamomile tea
How does that scent make you feel?
Lavender
Rose
And verivert, too
(What's verivert?)

Let's play a game about…smelling?
Think about it
It's sure to be fun!
Imagine the smell of fresh-cut grass
Doesn't that smell green?

Breathe in…what does that smell
    remind you of?
Try another one
Breathe in…what does that smell
    remind you of?
Which one do you like better?

Lois's Circle Form

THE NOSE KNOWS (continued)

Our nose knows so many things
How to smell cookies or mornings
   in spring
Our nose knows so many things
Let's all enjoy them now!

Have you ever thought about...
   smelling?
Well think about it!
It's kind of fun
Imagine the smell of chocolate...yum!
Doesn't that smell good...?
Think about it...

NOTE *"Vetivert," sometimes pronounced "verivert," as we do here, is the essential oil of the vetiver plant. The roots of this grass (native to India) yield an oil, the aroma of which is generally considered calming.*

Love and Kindness

RUN TIME 3 minutes, 30 seconds	**ARRANGEMENT BY** Wiz
VOCALS & MUSIC BY Bob Wiz—piano and synthesizer.	

This is quiet-time song.

Variations:
- ♪ Use this song to explore movements: stretching; reaching back, up, out, and forward; and bending down.
- ♪ Twirl with scarves or streamers.
- ♪ Begin by sitting on the floor, then gradually stand upright.
- ♪ This Songame can be preceded by a drawing activity: Draw something or someone that makes you feel loving and kind. Talk about the drawings after dancing the feelings of loving and kindness. Yes, we believe this is a good thing for both girls and boys to do. You may wish to post the pictures or send them home with the kids so parents will know what makes their children feel warm and cozy.
- ♪ If used as a quiet-time song, you may want to encourage the children to use the time to be loving and kind with themselves. Even better, take a break and do this introspective activity with them—we can all use it!

Lois's Circle Form

Aubrey's Circle Form

"Sensory modulation is the tendency to generate responses that are graded in relation to incoming sensation" (Lai et al). Kids who struggle with generating the "right" response to incoming sensations can have a difficult time in situations that demand a high frequency of correct responses to incoming sensations.

As we mentioned in the introduction, a child is not supposed to freak out when he hears the bell to change classes or have a meltdown if his orange juice has too much pulp in it! But the kids we love often have a difficult time generating the right response to certain types of stimuli because their perception of incoming sensations is different. Sounds are too loud or too soft; smells are too strong or too weak. Some children even have difficulty knowing exactly where their body is in space because their relationship to gravity is challenged.

Aubrey's circle form is intended to help children experience different musical inputs and translate the cues into graded responses (actions). This is the perfect circle form to try with kids who tend to be overresponsive to incoming sensation. The circle form flows from big playful movement, creativity, and innovation to a slower, more peaceful and relaxing state.

RUN TIME 20 minutes, 6 seconds

Glider Rider

RUN TIME 5 minutes, 35 seconds	ARRANGEMENT BY Freeman/Burhoe
VOCALS & MUSIC BY Ravi Freeman—kora. Ty Burhoe—tabla.	

Glide out of naptime to fuss-free wake-up play!

Variations:

♪ The gliding softness at the beginning helps the child to wake up gently. The more punctuated tabla (drum) sounds are a gentle way to help kids wake up their minds.

♪ Use imagery. Have the child lie down in a comfortable place with his eyes closed, with natural light or with lights dimmed, and imagine flying, swimming, or gliding. If you like, you can have the child describe to you what he or she "sees."

If the child is at a loss for images, you may suggest different landscapes, such as flying over mountains, cities, towns, forests, deserts, oceans, or Antarctica. What does he see when he flies up high or swoops down low? This is a great way to promote imaginative play and an easy way for a child to "write" a story! You can even take notes and help him work them into a story later.

Or, if you have a tape recorder you can record the session, with the child speaking and "Glider Rider" playing in the background. If the child likes the recording, you can send it home with him. (*Hint:* If you don't make a big deal about recording, he or she is sure to be less self-conscious.)

Aubrey's Circle Form

Fine-Motor Samba

RUN TIME 2 minutes, 59 seconds   **VOCALS & MUSIC BY** Aubrey Lande—vocals. Art Lande—piano.
Based on "One Note Samba," by Antonio Carlos Jobim. Used with permission. **ADAPTATION BY** Lande/Lande.

Eliminate tension! Shaking out the stress makes fine-motor movements become more graceful and easier to do. Body tension unwinds to allow easy movements and more comfortable balance, as well as expression through the shoulders, arms, legs, ankles, wrists, toes, fingers, and the nose. Encourage playful drawing to the rhythm of the music.

Variations:

- ♪ Use scarves or pompons while doing the movements.
- ♪ Have your child name body parts as he or she stretches while waking up.
- ♪ Deep pressure to the feet, hands, shoulders, knees, and head can offer a gentle transition from drowsiness to wakefulness.
- ♪ Have the child stretch high up and wide when "drawing" the song. You could add targets for the child to reach toward.
- ♪ Finger-paint or use chalk to draw the song on paper or the sidewalk to increase sensory awareness.

So, take your hands and shake them
Wake them up and wiggle them
Make fists and then release them
Again, again, again
Get your shoulders ready
Lift them up and let them down
Now put your arms in front of you
And draw this sound
(musical interlude)

Conduct the music gently
Or like Leonard Bernstein would
With passion, strength, dimension
Any way you play is good
Now have a pen and paper ready
We're gonna draw a picture now
Let your fingers do the "listening"
And draw this sound!
(musical interlude)

Ankles, wrists, and noses
Love to play this game
So use your imagination
And you'll never be the same.

Aubrey's Circle Form **63**

Give a Little Yodel

| **RUN TIME** 2 minutes, 29 seconds | **ARRANGEMENT BY** Lande/Lande |

Medley with Malcom Arnold. Used with permission. **VOCALS & MUSIC BY** Aubrey Lande—vocals. Art Lande—piano. Mark Miller—flute. Bob Wiz—yodeler.

Here's a new and positive way of changing from sluggishness to alert attention through rhythmic play.

Variation:
Have your child use different sounds to let you know how he or she is feeling—for example, a "little yodel" when happy, clapping hands when grumpy, or tapping feet or fingers when sad.

Bears wake from hibernation
But they're cranky as can be
If only they would yodel *(repeat this line)*
They moan and groan and forage but they don't wake easily. With a little yodel they would *(repeat this line)*

Brown bears daydream
Grizzlies bake
It's pandemonium when they're just half-awake
So when you're beary sleepy
Beary groggy and confused
Growl and howl and yodel
And march around the room

(The marching theme in the interlude is "The Colonel Bogey March" from "Bridge Over the River Kwai")

Bears wake from hibernation
And they're cranky as can be
If only they would yodel *(repeat this line)*
They moan and groan and growl and forage but they don't wake easily
With a little yodel they would
With a little yodel they would

Brown bears daydream
Grizzlies bake
It's pandemonium when they're just half-awake
So when you're beary sleepy
Beary groggy and confused
Growl and howl and yodel
And march around your room!

Slowing Down

RUN TIME 2 minutes, 39 seconds **ARRANGEMENT BY** Lande/Wiz
VOCALS & MUSIC BY Aubrey Lande—vocals. Bob Wiz—drum machine and keyboard.

This song takes the shock out of the command to "SETTLE DOWN!" It starts where the child's energy is and gradually guides him or her to a more organized, calm state.

Variations:

♪ Use this Songame after recess, at bedtime, at naptime, or whenever everyone seems out of control.
♪ Use it when a storm is coming in!
♪ Pretend you're a robot and slow down. Pretend that your batteries are really low and you have to slow down before you just stop. Slow your movements and your speech.

Slowing down
Slowing down
Everybody's slowing down

(These lyrics are repeated at slower and slower rhythms until the end of the Songame.)

Aubrey's Circle Form **65**

Mama Loves Me

RUN TIME 5 minutes, 53 seconds	**TRADITIONAL ARRANGEMENT BY** Lande/Cunningham/Davies
VOCALS & MUSIC BY Aubrey Lande—vocals. Cindy Cunningham—mbira. Roberta Davies—mbira.	

This song is based on a traditional African piece called "Karige Mombé." Here it is used as a transition, calming, or wake-up song.

Variations:

- ♫ Sit or stand in a circle, with your arms around each other's shoulders, and sway with the beat.
- ♫ Sing with the music.
- ♫ At quiet time, use this song to slow down.
- ♫ Lie in a circle with your heads together and hum with the music.
- ♫ Use with headphones at an appropriate volume.
- ♫ Create a cozy listening environment with blankets and pillows.

Hahhh maaa luhhz oohhh
(These lyrics are repeated for the entire Songame.)

References

1. Anderson E, Emmons P. *Unlocking the Mysteries of Sensory Integration.* Arlington, TX: Future Horizons; 1996.

2. Ayres AJ. *Sensory Integration and Learning Disorders.* Los Angeles, CA: Western Psychological Services; 1972.

3. Ayres AJ. The Sensory Integration and Praxis Tests. Los Angeles, CA: Western Psychological Services; 1989.

4. Sensorimotor foundations of academic ability. In: Cruickshank WM, Hallahan DP. *Perceptual and Learning Disabilities in Children.* Vol 2. Syracuse, NY: Syracuse University Press; 1975:301-358.

5. Ayres AJ. *Sensory Integration and the Child.* Los Angeles, CA: Western Psychological Services; 1979.

6. Bissell J, Fisher J, Owens C, Polcyn P. *Sensory Motor Handbook: A Guide for Implementing and Modifying Activities in the Classroom.* Torrance, CA: Sensory Integration International; 1988.

7. Bonder BR, Fisher AG. Sensory integration and treatment of the elderly. *Gerontol Spec Interest Q.* 1989;12(1):2-4.

8. Brewer C, Campbell D. *Rhythms of Learning.* Phoenix, AZ: Zephyr Press; 1991.

9. Cermak SA. Developmental dyspraxia. In: Roy EA, ed. *Neuropsychological Studies of Apraxia and Related Disorders.* New York, NY: Elsevier; 1985:225-250.

10. Cermak S, Groza V. Sensory integration in post-institutionalized children: implications for social workers. *Child Adolesc Soc Work J.* 1998;16:5-37.

11. Clark F, Mailloux Z, Parham D. Sensory integration and children with learning disabilities. In: Pratt PN, Allen AS, eds. *Occupational Therapy for Children.* 2nd ed. St Louis, MO: C.V. Mosby; 1989:457-507.

12. Cohn E, Cermak S. Research outcome measures in sensory integration. *Am J Occup Ther.* 1998;52(7): 540-546.

13. DeGangi GA, Brienbauer C. The symptomatology of infants and toddlers with regulatory disorders. *J Dev Learning Disord.* 1997;1(1):183-213.

14. Dunn W. The impact of sensory processing abilities on the daily lives of young children and their families: a conceptual model. *Infants Young Child.* 1997;9(4):23-25.

15. Fisher AG, Murray EA, Bundy AC. *Sensory Integration: Theory and Practice.* Philadelphia, PA: F.A. Davis Company; 1991.

16. Gardner H. *Frames of Mind: The Theory of Multiple Intelligences.* New York, NY: Basic Books; 1993.

17. Grandin T. *Thinking in Pictures.* New York, NY: Doubleday; 1995.

18. Grandin T, Scariano M. *Emergence Labeled Autistic.* Novato, CA: Arena; 1986.

REFERENCES (continued)

19. Greenspan SI, Greenspan NT. *First Feelings: Milestones in the Emotional Development of Your Child from Birth to Age Four.* New York, NY: Viking Penguin; 1985.

20. Greenspan SI, Greenspan NT. *The Essential Partnership: How Parents Can Meet the Emotional Challenges of Infancy and Childhood.* New York, NY: Viking Penguin; 1989.

21. Greenspan SI, Salmon J. *The Challenging Child.* Reading, MA: Addison-Wesley Publishing Co; 1995.

22. Greenspan SI, Salmon J. *Playground Politics: Understanding the Emotional Life of Your School-Age Child.* Reading, MA: Addison-Wesley; 1993.

23. Greenspan SI, Wieder S, Simons R. *The Child with Special Needs.* Reading, MA: Addison-Wesley; 1998.

24. Kashman N, Mora J. *The Sensory Connection.* Las Vegas, NV: Sensory Resources; 2005.

25. Kranowitz CS. *The Out-of-Sync Child.* 2nd ed. New York, NY: Perigee Books; 2005.

26. Kranowitz CS. *The Out-of-Sync Child Has Fun.* New York, NY: Perigee Books; 2003.

27. Lai JS, Parham D, Johnson-Ecker C. Sensory dormancy and sensory defensiveness: two sides of the same coin? *Sensory Integration Special Interest Section Q.* Dec 1999;22:1-4.

28. Oetter P, Richter E, Frick S. *M.O.R.E. Integrating the Mouth with Sensory and Postural Functions.* 2nd ed. Hugo, MN: PDP Press; 1993.

29. Orth JE. Regulatory disorders and patterns of attachment in infancy and early childhood. *J Dev Learning Disord.* 1998;2(1).

30. Price S, Price L. *Aromatherapy for Health Professionals.* UK: Churchill Livingstone Publishing; 1993.

31. Schore A. *Affect Regulation and the Origin of the Self: The Neurobiology of Emotional Development.* Mahwah, NJ: Lawrence Erlbaum Associates; 1998.

32. Seiderman AS, Marcus SE. *20/20 Is Not Enough: The New World of Vision.* New York, NY: Fawcett Crest; 1991.

33. Silver LB. *The Misunderstood Child: A Guide for Parents of Children with Learning Disabilities.* 2nd ed. Blue Ridge Summit, PA: TAB Books; 1992.

34. Silver LB. Dr. *Larry Silver's Advice to Parents on Attention-Deficit Hyperactivity Disorder.* Washington, DC: American Psychiatric Press; 1993.

35. Szklut S, Cermak S, Henderson A. Learning disabilities. In: Umphred D, ed. *Neurological Rehabilitation.* 3rd ed. New York, NY: Mosby; 1995:312-359.

36. Trott MC, Laurel M, Windeck SL. *SenseAbilities: Understanding Sensory Integration.* San Antonio, TX: Therapy Skill Builders; 1993.

37. Vail PL. *Words Fail Me: How Language Works and What Happens When It Doesn't.* Rosemont, NJ: Modern Learning Press; 1996.

38. Wilbarger P, Wilbarger J. *Sensory Defensiveness in Children Ages 2-12: An Intervention Guide for Parents*

and Other Caretakers. Denver, CO: Avanti Education Products; 1990.

39. Williams MS, Shellenberger S. Introduction to "How Does Your Engine Run?" The Alert Program for Self-Regulation. Albuquerque, NM: Therapyworks; 1992.

39. Williams MS, Shellenberger S. How Does Your Engine Run? A Leader's Guide to the Alert Program for Self-Regulation. Albuquerque, NM: Therapyworks; 1994.

40. Worwood VA. The Complete book of Essential Oils and Aromatherapy. San Rafael, CA: New World Library; 1991.

41. Yack M, Sutton S, Aquilla P. Building Bridges through Sensory Integration. 2nd ed. Las Vegas, NV: Sensory Resources; 2003.

42. Zero to Three/National Center for Clinical Infant Programs. Diagnostic Classification of Mental Health and Developmental Disorders of Infancy and Early Childhood. Arlington, VA; 1995.

43. Kranowitz CS. The Goodenoughs Get in Sync. Arlington, TX: Sensory World; 2010.

Glossary

Attention-deficit disorder (ADD): A neurological problem that affects attention. At times, the child may be distracted by everything around him or her, while at other times, he or she may have an unrelenting drive to engage in preferred activities for long periods of time. The child with ADD may be impulsive and easily frustrated. In addition, if the child just can't stop fidgeting and moving, the problem is called attention-deficit/hyperactivity disorder, or ADHD. True ADD often coexists with other mood or regulatory disorders. Going the extra mile to discern the extent to which a child's skills might be affected is extremely important.

Auditory defensiveness: Noises, or even certain people's voices, can range from annoying to painful. Some children will cover their ears when they hear what they perceive to be irritating sounds.

Disinhibition: Some people are unable, or inconsistently able, to screen out unimportant sensory information. Disinhibition of the screening mechanism of the brain (see *Inhibition*) can feel almost intolerable. One child described how he felt on being unable to filter out this bombardment of sensory information. He said, "There's a traffic jam in my head."

Dyspraxia: This subcategory of SPD involves difficulty with learning the steps in a new skill and trouble performing this skill smoothly and automatically. Tying shoelaces, dressing, and mealtime skills may be difficult for a child with dyspraxia to acquire and refine. Often, the child can do a skill easily one day and be unable to do it the next day. After throwing a ball well, one child commented, "How did I DO that?"

Fight, flight, or freeze response: Problems with this response can mean responding to ordinary, everyday happenings (not just raging bulls and speeding trucks) as if they were life threatening. The child may respond by fighting, running away, or being so panicked he can't move. This response is the behavioral by-product of our autonomic nervous system response to a real or perceived threat.

Filtering: This is an instinctive, preconscious skill that makes it possible to scan the environment and selectively screen out nonessential or distracting sensory information.

Gravitational insecurity: Fear of being off the ground, sometimes to the extent of panicking. If severe, a person may feel that he is falling if his head is tipped back. Children with this problem

often have poor integration of the senses in the inner ear, muscles, and joints, which are so vital in maintaining a good relationship with gravity. (See *Proprioception* and *Vestibular system*.)

IDEA: The Individuals with Disabilities Education Act, PL 99-457, and amendments. This law states that school districts must provide occupational therapy for students identified as requiring services to address educational performance needs.

Inhibition: There is so much going on around us all the time that our nervous systems couldn't possibly handle it all without malfunctioning. Inhibition is a critical function of the nervous system, whereby the brain filters out useless information so we can focus. (See *Disinhibition*.) Certain activities can provide the nervous system with body-based ways of calming and organizing, such as doing push-ups, bicycling, or running. (See *Sensory diet*.) A person's "sensory diet" can incorporate some activities to assist the brain with inhibition and prevent sensory overload.

Learning disorder: Challenges with learning to read, write, or do math that can't be accounted for by straightforward problems with vision or hearing or by lack of exposure to educational programs. Alternative educational approaches are often needed, tailored to play to the child's strengths as a means of engaging the child in successful learning experiences.

Modulation: The ability of the nervous system to have a "middle ground" or "comfort zone" of regulation as a person interacts with the challenges of daily life. A child with SPD may have poor modulation, with a narrow "comfort zone."

Overresponsivity: Acute awareness of the environment, sometimes to the point of pain. Although one sense may be more sensitive to the environment than another, there is frequently overresponsivity in most of the basic senses: smell, touch, movement, vision, and hearing. A person who is overresponsive may display avoidance or strong aversions.

Praxis: The fluent synchrony of thought and movement, resulting in organized, intentional action. Purposeful movement is praxis in action. When someone has a well-developed sense of praxis, his or her intuitive understanding of how to move or manipulate objects reflects this fluent synchrony of thought and action. People who are dyspraxic, or lack a well-developed sense of praxis, will often develop compensatory thinking strategies that require much more thought, planning, and organization to accomplish novel movement tasks.

Proprioception: This term combines the Latin word *proprio*, which translates to "one's own," and the English word *receptive*. It is the awareness of ourselves gained through muscles and joints and through other receptors within our bodies.

Sensory diet: An individual's specific "inhibition" or "facilitation" activities strategically planned throughout the day to deal with stress, keeping the nervous system in a state of balance. (See *Modulation*.) Inhibition activities provide the nervous system with body-based ways of calming and organizing. Learning to self-assess and take activities for the appropriate action to bring one's nervous system into a balanced state is an essential feature of the sensory-diet concept.

GLOSSARY (continued)

Sensory discrimination: Taking in information through all our senses, then processing, filtering, and interpreting all these sensations with our bodies and minds as a base for developing skills.

Sensory processing: The process of taking in information about the world around us with all our senses and from inside our own bodies. Through integrating and organizing these senses of vision, touch, movement, muscle sense, hearing, taste, and smell, we are able to interact comfortably and efficiently in work and play and in caring for ourselves and others.

Sensory Processing Disorder (SPD): The inability of the brain to correctly process information brought in by the senses. We use sensory information to organize our behavior and successfully interact with the world. Our senses give us information about the physical status of our bodies and our environment. People with SPD misinterpret everyday sensory information, such as touch, sound, and movement. When anyone's perceptions of sensation are unreliable or inconsistent, he or she does not feel secure and safe, which can significantly affect behavior and functioning. People with SPD often have difficulty with everyday tasks, such as schoolwork, dressing, bathing, eating, sleeping, interacting with peers, and riding in cars. Treating SPD improves learning and behavior.

Tactile: Another word for "touch." Touch can be basic awareness of where and how a person has been touched, or it can involve more discriminative touch as a base for the development of skills.

Tactile defensiveness: Responding to light or unexpected touch as if it were uncomfortable or threatening. An overresponsivity to touch can interfere with relating comfortably to other people. A child with tactile defensiveness may object to having tags in his shirts, wearing "tickly" clothing, having his hair washed or teeth brushed, or handling certain textures. A person with tactile defensiveness may be sensitive to other sensations, as well, and always "on the defensive."

Underresponsivity: A "muffled" or dampened sensory awareness of the environment. This diminished sensory perception manifests as an unusually high tolerance for typically aversive stimuli, such as acute pain or loud noise. To truly assess underresponsivity, pathological causes, such as nerve damage, must be ruled out.

Vestibular system: The sensory system with receptors in the inner ear. It responds to changes in head position to help us keep our balance. This system is constantly "checking in" with our eyes, muscles, and joints to keep us oriented to gravity and to how we balance and move our bodies.

Resources

Organizations and Products

Sensory World

Sensory World, a proud division of Future Horizons, is the world's largest publisher devoted exclusively to resources for those interested in Sensory Processing Disorder (SPD). They also sponsor national conferences for parents, teachers, therapists, and others interested in supporting those with SPD. Visit *www.sensoryworld.com* for further information.

Sensory World
1010 N Davis Dr
Arlington, TX 76012
Phone: (877) 775-8968 or
(682) 558-8941
Fax: (682) 558-8945
info@sensoryworld.com
www.sensoryworld.com

Sensory products include *Insights into Sensory Issues for Professionals, Answers to Questions Teachers Ask about Sensory Integration, The Goodenoughs Get in Sync, The Sensory Connection, Prechool SENSE, Starting Sensory Therapy, MoveAbout Cards, 28 Instant Songames, Songames for Sensory Integration, Danceland, Marvelous Mouth Music, Making Sense of Sensory Integration, Eyegames, Sensory Parenting, Building Sensory Friendly Classrooms, Soothing the Senses, Learn to Have Fun with Your Senses,* and *Picky, Picky Pete.*

The Balzer-Martin Preschool Screening (BAPS)

Available from Saint Columba's Nursery School
4201 Albemarle St NW
Washington, DC 20016
(202) 363-4121
http://www.out-of-sync-child.com/pubsmore/balzer-martin.htm

This sensory-based program was developed by Dr Lynn Balzer-Martin, a highly regarded occupational therapist specializing in the assessment of children with sensory dysfunction. The Balzer-Martin Preschool Screening (BAPS) is used to help identify risk factors for learning and behavioral problems in children aged 3 to 5 years old.

Flaghouse, Inc

106 Flaghouse Dr
Hasbrouck, NJ 07664-3116
(800) 221-5185
www.flaghouse.com

This company carries products for children and adults with SPD. Flaghouse is especially well regarded for its environmental-enhancement products that facilitate calming and focusing on clients with moderate to severe issues.

RESOURCES (continued)

Future Horizons, Inc
721 W Abram St
Arlington, TX 76013
(800) 489-0727
Fax: (817) 277-2270
www.fhautism.com
Future Horizons is the world's largest publisher of books, DVDs, and other materials on autism, Asperger syndrome, and related disorders. They sponsor numerous conferences and workshops about autism and related disorders each year.

Henry OT Services
7924 W. Bell Rd, Ste C5-429
Glendale, AZ 85308
(623) 882-8812
Fax: (623) 877-1544
www.henryot.com
Diana Henry, OTR, has created several fine products, including the DVDs "Tools for Teachers" and "Tools for Students."

Mealtimes Catalog
New Visions
1124 Roberts Mountain Rd
Faber, VA 22938
(800) 606-7112 Ext. 10
www.new-vis.com
Offering mealtime activities and therapy materials, this is a wonderful resource for speech-language and oral-motor development, feeding concerns, and learning with music.

Optometric Extension Program Foundation, Inc (OEP)
1921 E Carnegie Ave, Ste 3-L
Santa Ana, CA 92705-5510
(949) 250-8070
Fax: (949) 250-8157
www.oepf.org
Offering products and information on workshops related to improving visual-motor skills.

PDP Products and Professional Development Programs
1675 Greeley St South, Ste 101
Stillwater, MN 55082
(877) 439-8865
www.pdppro.com
Generates developmental learning materials, sensory treatment products and publications, and continuing education seminars.

Pocket Full of Therapy
P.O. Box 174
Morganville, NJ 07747
(732) 441-0404 or (800) 736-8124
www.pfot.com
A unique collection of educational and therapeutic toys and materials for use in the clinic, at school, or at home.

Sensory Comfort Catalog
P.O. Box 6589
Portsmouth, NH 03802-6589
(888) 436-2622
www.sensorycomfort.com
This company specializes in making life more comfortable for children and adults with SPD.

Southpaw Enterprises
P.O. Box 1047
Dayton, OH 45401
(800) 228-1698
www.southpawenterprises.com
Offering therapy equipment and developmentally enriched toys for use at home, in school, or in the clinic.

Therapro, Inc
225 Arlington St
Framingham, MA 01702
(800) 257-5376
www.therapro.com
Developmental learning materials, sensory treatment products and publications, continuing education seminars.

Organizations

Administration on Developmental Disabilities
U.S. Department of Health and Human Services
200 Independence Ave SW, Rm 329D
Washington, DC 20201
(202) 690-6590
www.hrsa.gov
Here you can find information regarding federally funded programming specific to the prevention, diagnosis, and treatment of developmental disabilities.

The American Occupational Therapy Association, Inc (AOTA)
4720 Montgomery Ln
Bethesda, MD 20824-1220
(301) 652-2682
www.aota.org
This professional organization promotes improved public awareness of occupational-therapy services.

American Speech-Language-Hearing Association (ASHA)
2200 Research Blvd
Rockville, MD 20850-3289
Members: (800) 498-2071
Non-Member: (800) 638-8255
www.asha.org
Offering information about speech-therapy services, products, and publications, as well as referrals to therapists.

RESOURCES (continued)

Council for Exceptional Children (CEC)
1920 Association Dr
Reston, VA 20191
(866) 509-0218
www.cec.sped.org
A federally funded clearinghouse for information on special needs.

Developmental Delay Resources
5801 Beacon St
Pittsburgh, PA 15217
(800) 497-0944
Fax: (412) 422-1374
www.devdelay.org
A nonprofit organization dedicated to helping parents and professionals learn cutting-edge strategies to help children with special needs. Their membership directory is a comprehensive resource for networking parents and professionals interested in complementary treatment approaches, and they publish a very useful newsletter.

Learning Disabilities Association of America (LDA)
4156 Library Rd
Pittsburgh, PA 15234
(412) 341-1515
www.ldanatl.org
A professional organization that advocates on behalf of people with learning disabilities.

Mozart Effect Resource Center
P.O. Box 800
Boulder, CO 80306-0800
(303) 938-1188
www.mozarteffect.com
This organization sponsors seminars on creative ways to use music to facilitate learning. In addition, it circulates a product catalog with lots of interesting resources for using music at home, at school, or in therapy. This organization is affiliated with MMB Music, the publishers of the MMB Catalog of creative arts therapy and general music education. Materials by Mozart Effect author Don Campbell are available from this organization.

National Information Center for Children and Youth with Disabilities (NICHCY)
1825 Connecticut Ave NW, Ste 700
Washington, DC 20009
(800) 695-0285
www.nichcy.org
A clearinghouse for resource information on raising children with special needs.

Parent Network for the Post-Institutionalized Child (PNPIC)
www.adoption-research.org
A parent-centered support and resource referral organization for parents who have adopted post-institutionalized children.

Therapy Works, Inc
7200 Montgomery NE, Ste B9, Box 397
Albuquerque, NM 87109
Toll-free: (877) 897-3478 always open
www.alertprogram.com
This group offers workshops on helping parents and professionals learn about SPD and its effects on self-regulation skills. Therapy Works' cofounders, Mary Sue Williams, MS, OTR/L, and Sherry Shellenberger, MS, OTR/L, developed a treatment model for children that is widely regarded as an effective method of teaching children how to assess and change their level of self-regulation through specific kinds of movement and sensory play activities. *The Alert Program with Songs for Self Regulation* outlines this program.

Zero to Three/National Center for Clinical Infant Programs
1255 23rd St NW, Ste 350
Washington, DC 20037
(202) 638-1144
www.zerotothree.org
The publisher of *Zero to Three* magazine, this educational organization is geared toward training parents and professionals to encourage the physical, emotional, social, and cognitive growth of children aged 0-3.

Web Resources
To find a qualified occupational or physical therapist or other service provider in your area, please visit:

Sensory Processing Disorder Foundation
5655 S. Yosemite St, Ste 305
Greenwood Village, CO 80111
(303) 794-1182
www.spdnetwork.org
The Sensory Processing Disorder Foundation... expanding knowledge, fostering awareness and promoting recognition of Sensory Processing Disorder

www.out-of-sync-child.com
Carol Kranowitz the worlds leading authority on Understanding Sensory Processing Disorder.

www.npnd.org
The mission of the National Parent Network on Disabilities (NPND) is to provide a presence and national voice for ALL families of children, youth and adults with disabilities.

Have Fun with Other Songames Sets!
at www.sensoryworld.com

Each Songames™ CD contains fun musical activities for improving fine- and gross-motor skills, muscle strength, and rhythmicity. These musical gems are useful for engaging kids in active games, as well as helping kids calm down and focus. Songames are great for enhancing oral-motor skills and expressive language play and decreasing tactile, auditory, visual, and sensory defensiveness. Kids will want to play Songames over and over again!

Includes CD
+ 48-page booklet.

28 Instant Songames™
Fun-Filled Activities for Kids 3-8
by Barbara Sher, MS, OTR

Twenty-eight games that make children feel good about themselves—what could be more fun than that?? Winner of the 2000 Oppenheim Toy Portfolio SNAP Award and Dr. Toy's Best Vacation Children's Products, *28 Instant Songames* is great fun for typically developing children, as well as those with special needs!

This full-length, 28-song music CD will get kids up and moving in no time. The activities include numerous games of body awareness, movement play, feeling identification, and self-expression, as well as imagination games that encourage expressive language play. **These less complex Songames and activities are perfect for younger children.**

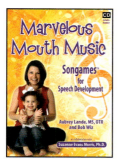

Includes CD
+ 55-page booklet.

Marvelous Mouth Music
Songames™ for Speech Development
by Suzanne Evans Morris, PhD, CCC-SLP

Marvelous Mouth Music is an audio CD of 21 activity-based Songames designed by Dr Suzanne Evans Morris, an internationally recognized speech therapist. **Ideally suited for kids age 2 years to those with fully developed speech**, this CD brings speech development to life through musical play. Instrumentation includes guitar, mandolin, dulcimer, drums, synthesizer, and percussion.

The 55-page companion booklet includes a "How to Use" section, song lyrics, a model for how to use all types of music to promote therapeutic change, and a glossary of important terms written in easy-to-understand, parent-centered language.

Danceland
Songames™ and Activities to Improve Sensory Skills
by Kristen Fitz Taylor, RPT, and Cheryl McDonald, RPT

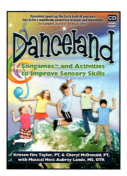

Danceland is a musical invitation to move joyfully and creatively! **Designed for slightly older children, ages 5-12**, the music invites participation and engages children in rhythmic expression, which is fundamental to physical, cognitive, and emotional development. Designed by physical and occupational therapists, more than 75 movement activities can be adapted for physical education and home programming.

The "travel guide" combines theory with instruction, while encouraging you to put your own creative twists on the activities. Turn dances into games, choreographed stories, or theatrical performances! Polka to an authentic Krakowiak or have kids choreograph their own movements to singer Lora Dart's Native American song, "Touch the Earth." Kids can croon karaoke-style to an uproarious remake of the 60s hit, "Wild Thing," or have a Kwanzaa party to "Wisdom of Africa." The possibilities are endless!

Includes CD
+ 28-page booklet.

Soothing the Senses
15 Lyrical Selections to Soothe and Relax
Fred Hersch

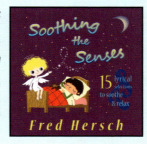

Award-winning pianist Fred Hersch plays 15 luxuriously gentle and lyrical selections to relax and soothe the senses. The CD features compositions from Hersch, as well as Debussy, Mozart, Bach, and Gershwin. The accompanying leaflet features tips and resources for caregivers.

About the Authors

Aubrey Lande, MS, OTR, received her MS degree in occupational therapy from Boston University and subsequently worked for The Children's Hospital of Denver. A recipient of a healthcare leadership postgraduate fellowship from the University of Colorado Medical Center, Aubrey combines her many years of clinical work as a pediatric occupational therapist with her chops as a singer, composer, and visual artist. She and her husband, musician Art Lande, teach musical and movement strategies for self-regulation in Boulder, Colorado, and beyond. To find out more, visit their sound gallery at www.ConsciousSensoryProcessing.Org.

Art Lande lives in Boulder, Colorado. He composes and teaches music and performs all around the globe. Visit www.ArtLande.com for more information.

AUBREY & ART LANDE

Bob Wiz is a composer, teacher, musician, producer, arranger, and recording engineer. He received his BA degree in Mass Media Communication from Cleveland State University and has since become a beloved figure in the musical landscape of Boulder, Colorado. Bob teaches creative music to individuals and groups by using techniques garnered from a lifelong interest in the performing arts. Bob is a freelance producer with a special interest in projects relating to meditation and mind-body awareness. Currently, he collaborates with vocalist Danae Shanti, producing a series of breath-based meditations. Bob also creates eclectic, soulful world music with the band TrioTribe. He continues to teach creative piano, to create healing music and art, and to perform in the Boulder area. Learn more at www.RadiantRhythms.com.

BOB WIZ

Lois Hickman, MS, OTR, FAOTA is an occupational therapist who has been practicing in the Boulder, Colorado, area since 1972. She has practiced in both hospital and clinical settings and has lectured nationally and internationally on sensory integration, the utilization of music and story in occupational therapy, and the application of occupational therapy in therapeutic horseback riding. Currently, her private practice with children and adults has encompassed clinical work, farming, and therapeutic horseback riding. She enjoys collaborating with clients, families, and other professionals on ways to incorporate fun (including musical fun) into the often-serious business of therapy.

LOIS HICKMAN